COME TO THE WATER BROOK

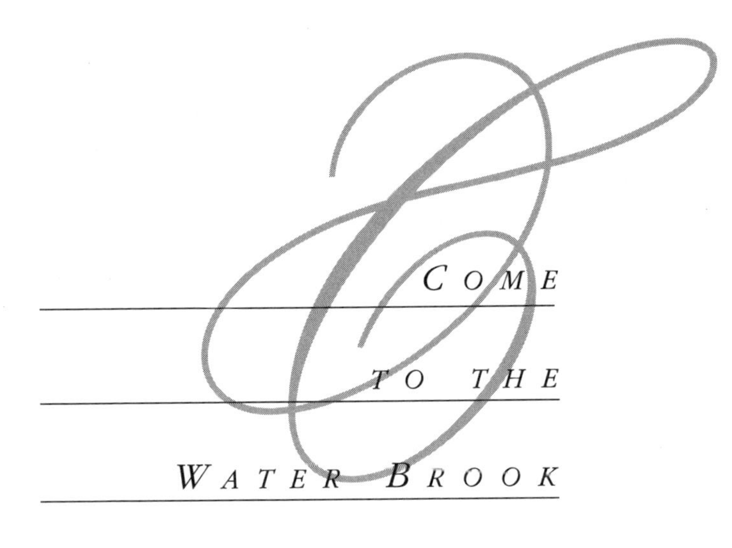

Come to the Water Brook

Stories, Songs, and Scriptures for Thirsty Souls

Written and Selected by
NEIL B. WISEMAN

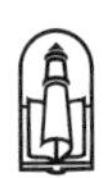

Beacon Hill Press of Kansas City
Kansas City, Missouri

ISBN 083-411-7037

Printed in the
United States of America

Cover Design: Kevin Williamson
Cover Photo: Japack Company / Westlight

Library of Congress Cataloging-in-Publication Data

Wiseman, Neil B.

Come to the water brook : stories, songs, and scripture for thirsty souls / compiled by Neil B. Wiseman.

p. cm.

ISBN 0-8341-1703-7 (pb)

1. Christian life—Meditations. I. Title

BV4501.2.W57416 1998

242—dc21 97-35070

CIP

10 9 8 7 6 5 4 3 2 1

Contents

Acknowledgments

The publisher and author gratefully acknowledge permission to use these stories:

"Don't Expect Too Much"
Vance Havner, *In Tune with Heaven,* Baker Book House, 1990.

"A Sense of Wonder Transforms Behavior"
Bill Moyers, *A World of Ideas.* Copyright © 1989 by Public Affairs Television, Inc. Used by permission of Doubleday, a division of Bantam Doubleday Dell Publishing Group, Inc.

"Real Success Is a Spiritual Experience"
From *Dear You* by Donald Russell Robertson, 1989, Word, Inc., Dallas, Texas. All rights reserved. Used by permission.

"What I Learned at Little League"
From *Turned On* by Roger Dow and Susan Cook, 1996. Reprinted by permission of HarperCollins Publishers, Inc.

"Wherever—The Adventure of the Quest"
From *In Quest of the Shared Life* by Bob Benson, 1981. Copyright © Solitude and Celebration Press, Nashville, Tennessee, assigned to Bob Benson, 1984. Used by permission.

"On Saying Grace"
"God Loves Eccentricity and Excitement"
"An Army That Keeps Transforming the World"
"The Seeker Whistled His Way to God"
From William G. Harris, *Stuff That Makes an Army,* Alexandria, Va.: The Salvation Army Press, 1962.

"Serving Always Connects Us to Jesus"
From *Something Beautiful for God: Mother Teresa of Calcutta* by Malcolm Muggeridge. Copyright © 1971 by The Mother Teresa Committee. Reprinted by permission of HarperCollins Publishers, Inc.

"The Power of Little People"
From *The Wisdom of the Elders* by Robert Fleming, Ballantine Books, 1996. Used by permission of Random House, Inc.

"The Clash of Hopes"
From *The Power of Hope* by Maurice Lamm, Rawson Associates, 1995. Used by permission of Maurice Lamm.

Your soul suffers
if you live superficially.

—ALBERT SCHWEITZER

1
Living a Christ-Quality Life

Cherry Pies and Excellence

As a young, part-time faculty member in a newly organized college, I was filled with idealism and lofty aspirations. So I dared to speak in a faculty meeting about an issue I thought we could improve with little effort and make a big difference in our work. But I misread the signals. The dean, proud of what had been accomplished, replied to my suggestion, "Don't you ever forget how far we have come in such a short period of time."

Thinking improvement would be welcomed, especially the kind that cost nothing, I was crushed. But I clearly understood the unspoken communication from our leader that I was to keep my peace and rejoice in the advances we had already made. So I dropped the issue. I kept quiet as my leader wished, but not without passive inner resistance.

The next day, while having lunch with a couple in their middle 70s who were giving their time for one dollar per year to the new college, I asked, "How old do you have to be before you stop looking forward?"

My friend Audrey caught my message immediately and replied, "Much older than I am."

Then she continued, "Tomorrow, I plan to bake a cherry pie. It will be the best cherry pie I have ever baked. It will have a tad more shortening, a better brand of cherries; and I'll bake it for a few more minutes than my last cherry pie."

She hesitated for just a moment and then continued, "How many cherry pies have I baked in my life? Hundreds, I guess, but every one has been a preparation for the next cherry pie." She hesitated again, then said, "Tomorrow's cherry pie will be the best I have ever made, and the pie after that will be a little better still."

That's the way Audrey taught her classes and the way she lived and the way she led women's conferences and the way she wrote books too. It's an invigorating challenge for every sphere of life, for the routines of life, for the repetitions of life, for the relationships of life.

Celebrate God all day, every day. I mean, *revel* in him!

—*Phil. 4:4*

It Is Well

With uncanny realism, W. D. McGraw, my friend and father-in-law, planned his own funeral. Simply because he realized it was the last changing of the seasons for him and because the Christian faith was his lodestar, he recorded a solo to be played at his funeral. On a cassette recording, he sang us a song of strength. Though dead, we heard him sing:

When peace like a river attendeth my way,
When sorrows like sea billows roll,
Whatever my lot, Thou hast taught me to say,
"It is well, it is well with my soul."

Then he asked us to sing along with him:

And, Lord, haste the day when the faith shall be sight,
The clouds be rolled back as a scroll,
The trump shall resound and the Lord shall descend.
Even so—it is well with my soul.

—Horotio G. Spafford

Finally, he said something like, "Come on; I know you can do better. Let's increase the tempo and sing together again with more faith and hope."

Luther's Remedy for Discouragement

Luther always advised against any attempt to wrestle one's way through. "Don't argue with the devil," he said. "He has had five thousand years of experience. He has tried out all his tricks on Adam, Abraham, and David, and he knows exactly the weak spots."

And the devil is persistent. If he does not get you down with the first assault, he will commence a siege of attrition until you give in from sheer exhaustion. Better banish the whole subject. Seek company and discuss some irrelevant matters such as, for example, what is going on in Venice. Shun solitude. "Eve got into trouble when she walked in the garden alone. I have my worst temptations when I am by myself." Seek out some Christian brother, some wise counsel. Undergird yourself with the fellowship of the church. Then, too, seek convivial company, feminine company. Dine, joke, and sing. Make yourself eat and drink, even though food may be distasteful.

Once Luther gave three rules for dispelling despondency: the first is faith in Christ; the second is to get downright angry; the third is the love of a mate.

How to Sing Strength into Your Soul

Here are John Wesley's instructions for spiritual singing:

1. Learn to sing these tunes before you learn any others; afterwards learn as many as you please.

2. Sing these tunes exactly as they are printed, without altering or mending them at all; and if you have learned to sing them otherwise, unlearn it as soon as you can.

3. Sing all. See that you join with the congregation as frequently as you can. Let not a slight degree of weakness or weariness hinder you. If it is a cross to you, take it up, and you will find a blessing.

4. Sing lustily and with a good courage. Beware of singing as if you were half dead or half asleep; but lift up your voice with strength. Be no more afraid of your voice now nor more ashamed of its being heard than when you sang the songs of Satan.

5. Sing modestly. Do not bawl, so as to be heard above or distinct from the rest of the congregation, that you may not destroy the harmony; but strive to unite your voices together so as to make one clear melodious sound.

6. Sing in time. Whatever time is sung, be sure to

keep with it. Do not run before nor stay behind it; but attend close to the leading voices, and more therewith as exactly as you can; and take care not to sing too slowly. This drawling way naturally steals on all who are lazy; and it is high time to drive it out from us, and sing all our tunes just as quickly as we did at first.

7. Above all sing spiritually. Have an eye to God in every word you sing. Aim at pleasing Him more than yourself or any other creature. In order to do this, attend strictly to the sense of what you sing, and see that your heart is not carried away with the sound, but offered to God continually; so shall your singing be such as the Lord will approve here, and reward you when He comes in the clouds of heaven.

—From the Preface to *Sacred Melody,* 1761

We've been given a brand-new life and have everything to live for, including a future in heaven—and the future starts now! God is keeping careful watch over us and the future. The Day is coming when you'll have it all—life healed and whole.

—1 Pet. 1:3-5

I Can't Drown

My wife and I were on vacation together after our first year of pastoral ministry. We had retreated to Florida to soak up a lot of sun and to rest from the constant pressures and increased demands of a growing congregation.

While dealing with the normal adjustments in being newlyweds, we were also trying to cope with our call to full-time ministry. The ever-constant expectations of others and our inability to keep everyone satisfied had caused us to doubt our potential to really succeed in pastoral ministry.

While resting one afternoon on the hotel patio, I noticed a young boy in the deep end of the swimming pool. He was having a difficult time making it to the ladder to climb out of the water. In his combination dog paddle and butterfly stroke, he inched his way to the side of the pool, struggled up the ladder while gasping and coughing to catch his breath.

But to my amazement, he walked directly to the diving board, marched out to the end, and jumped into the deep water again to repeat the whole process. Of course, I was concerned for his safety, so I met him at the ladder before his third lap.

"Hi," I said nervously. "Looks like you're learning to swim."

"Yep," he said between his coughs.

"Don't you think it would be better to learn how to swim in the shallow end of the pool?" I asked. "After all, you could get tired, and it would be dangerous down here in this deep water."

"Oh, that's all right," he said as he made his way back to the diving board. "It's not that dangerous; besides, I *can't* drown."

As he walked out to the end of the board preparing to jump again, I said, "Wait a minute, son! You *can* drown. A lot of people who are older and stronger than you have drowned in pools no deeper than this. And many of them were great swimmers."

Then he looked at me with a confident smile. "Mister, you see that guy sitting over there reading the newspaper? He's my dad, and he's watching me while I learn how to swim. So you see, I really *can't* drown."

Maybe it was just the timing of that faith-filled response or the confidence in his face, but I left that young man with a new sense of God's watchful care over one pastor who felt he was in over his head. Many have been the times I've been reminded to trust my Heavenly Father and know while He's watching over me, I *can't* drown.

—*Jim Dorsey*

Don't Expect Too Much

There is such a thing as asking too much of life. Some of us have been too hard to please. We austerely demanded too much of everything and consequently do not receive enough of anything.

Do not demand too much of success. Success is a strange game; some get there while others as well qualified miss it. And those who arrive often find their greatness only a hollow mockery and wish they were back where you are.

Do not ask too much of people. Be prepared to be disappointed in the best and surprised in the worst of folks, and do not too easily censure others. Be tolerant of us mortals—none is so wretched but that in him or her dwells some spark of good; none so saintly but may sin.

Do not demand too much of love. Whether or not you live happily ever after will depend greatly on how much old-fashioned patience and tolerance and understanding you weave into your common experience.

Do not expect too much of religion, for that is no "Open Sesame" to all life's closed doors and knotty problems. While it is born of the Spirit and rooted in the mystical, it also is intensely practical, and God does not work *for* you as much as *through* you. Religion as a fair and rosy outlook upon life amounts to little, save as it is brought down into the daily grind and worked out in the commonplace world. God is no indulgent grandmother to grant the whims of every capricious child; He will go His mile as we go our inch. Don't count on your religion as a sort of soul insurance that looks after your eternal interests while you go about temporal concerns quite forgetful of it. Religion in a very true sense is what you make it.

In whatever realm you move—career, society, love, religion—do not ask too much of life. Don't be unreasonable; this is not the millennium. Remember you are in the world as it is, and it is a complicated mixture of puzzling lights and shadows that thrills here and disgusts there. Mix your enthusiasm with good sense, and temper your revulsions with sympathy.

Thus you will not be driven to despair on the one side or be easily fooled on the other. And if you do not expect too much of life, you will not be hopelessly disappointed.

—Vance Havner

[God] thought of everything, provided for everything we could possible need, letting us in on the plans he took such delight in making. He set it all out before us in Christ, a long-range plan in which everything would be brought together and summed up in him, everything in deepest heaven, everything on planet earth.

—Eph. 1:9-10

Get Ready for the Nudges of God

One of the glorious things about the Christian faith is that it is so warm and personal. Without denying the unbelievable vastness of the universe—in fact, our faith marvelously opens our hearts and minds to the wonders of creation and the never-endingness of space and time—our faith keeps our minds balanced and our hearts warm with a God of love who cherishes and guides us personally. He knows us by name and even has the hairs of our head numbered.

It seems simplistic, and many bright people think it is irrational to say it, but I believe that God has a plan for each of our lives.

Things don't just happen to us who love God.
They're planned by His own dear hand,
Then molded and shaped and timed by His clock;
Things don't just happen—they're planned.

But how do we know just what is the will of God for us now, today, tomorrow? First, we must enjoy the wonder of having a personal relationship with Him—we the limited, faulty creatures of His hand and He the infinite, holy, loving.

Then when we face significant choices, we survey all the facts and factors of our potential, our preparation, our obligations and relationships. We use our best judgment and listen to the whisper of our deepest longings. During all this, and then finally, fearfully, we wait for an assurance, a nudge from the Lord—His leading.

What a glorious way to live! He leadeth me! Oh, blessed thought! And to end life believing that in all the major choices and pathways, Jesus led me all the way.

—John E. Riley

O Hope of ev'ry contrite heart,
O Joy of all the meek,
To those who fall, how kind Thou art!
How good to those who seek!
—Bernard of Clairvaux

Take particular care in picking out your building materials. Eventually there is going to be an inspection. If you use cheap or inferior materials, you'll be found out. The inspection will be thorough and rigorous.

—1 Cor. 3:12-13

A Sense of Wonder Transforms Behavior

Jacob Needleman, professor of philosophy and comparative religion at San Francisco State University, in an interview with Bill Moyers, told this story:

"I was invited by *Time* magazine to be an observer at the launch of Apollo 17. At that time, there were a lot of cynical people complaining about the space program, that it was taking money away from the poor and all that. But I went down. It was a night launch, and there were hundreds and hundreds of reporters all over the lawn, drinking beer and waiting for this tall, 35-story-high white rocket lit by those powerful lamps. We were sitting around joking and wisecracking and listening to the voice of Walter Cronkite like the voice of God coming over the loudspeaker telling us what was going on.

"Then the countdown came, and then the launch. The first thing you see is this extraordinary orange light, which is just at the limit of light that you can bear to look at. You don't have to turn away. It's beautiful; everything's illuminated with this light. Then comes this slow thing rising up in total silence, because it takes a few seconds for the count to come across. Then you hear a '*Whoooooooh! Hhhhmmmm!*' It enters right into you. This extraordinary thing is lifting up. Suddenly, among all these cynical people and the wisecracking people, myself included, you could practically hear their jaws dropping. The sense of wonder fills everyone in the whole place, as this thing goes up and up and up and up. The first stage ignites this beautiful blue flame. It becomes like a star, but you realize there are human beings on it. And then there's total silence.

"Then people just get up quietly, helping each other up. They're kind. They open doors. They look at each other, speaking quietly and interestedly. These were sudden moral people because wonder, the sense of wonder, the experience of wonder, had made them moral.

"By the time we got back to the hotel, it was gone. But my point is, in the state of wonder, no one can commit a crime. When you're in touch with something inner, you just are naturally sharing and caring to other people. So to me, the pursuit of understanding ethics without trying to understand this inner self won't go past a certain point."

Moyers then asked, "You used the word 'moral' rather than 'ethical' for the moment of knowing and sharing. Why?"

Needleman replied, "'Ethics' refers to outer actions, what you do. But inwardly, you are moral. That is, you are in touch with something that's truer, more your right nature, your real nature. As a result, you act in a way that could be judged moral."

Think of the implications of cultivating this "sense of wonder" and "your own real nature" for transforming lives and revolutionizing human behavior.

My faith has found a resting place—
Not in device nor creed:
I trust the Ever-living One—
His wounds for me shall plead.

Enough for me that Jesus saves—
This ends my fear and doubt;
A sinful soul, I come to Him—
He'll never cast me out.

—Lidie H. Edmunds

Go out into the world uncorrupted, a breath of fresh air in this squalid and polluted society. Provide people with a glimpse of good living and of the living God.

—Phil. 2:15

Real Success Is a Spiritual Experience

A while ago when I was surfing the TV channels, I saw Merv Griffin interviewing Kirk Douglas. The famous actor described the poverty that had gripped his early life. He told of his struggle to find work and recognition in New York City. One incident particularly stuck with me.

One evening, Kirk Douglas and another aspiring young actor were sitting together in Central Park. Full of ambition and dreams, Douglas pointed to the top floor, the 25th, of a very expensive Manhattan hotel and said, "Someday I am going to live in the most expensive suite up there. I am going to be right up there where those lights are."

Then Kirk Douglas paused, and in his own distinctive, dramatic way, he spoke to Griffin and the television audience as though he was divulging a great secret or revelation. He said, "You know, as time went on, I did live up there in the best suite on the 25th floor. But when I lived there, I found it wasn't as much fun looking down on Central Park as it was being in the park looking up at the lights on the 25th floor."

I have heard this same theme and thought from

many other successful actors and actresses. They hoped, they dreamed, they worked to become stars. When they did "make it," there was not nearly the satisfaction they had expected.

Oh, perhaps at the first, the flush of "success" was exciting and exhilarating. But in the long run, they felt somehow empty; they felt that something was missing.

The reason for this is simple but often slippery: fame and money do not satisfy the deepest needs in our hearts. I do not mean to knock the desire for success. But real success is a spiritual experience.

—Donald Russell Robertson

Jesus! what a Guide and Keeper!
While the tempest still is high,
Storms about me, night o'ertakes me,
He, my Pilot, hears my cry.

—J. Wilbur Chapman

Your lives aren't small, but you're living them in a small way. . . . Open up your lives. Live openly and expansively!

—2 Cor. 6:12-13

Lessons from an Old Wood-carver

I was talking recently with an old wood-carver who carves wild ducks and other wild birds. "Tell me how you go about this," I asked.

"Well, I start with the belief that there's a duck hidden in this block of wood and it's my job to find it."

As we talked, he turned the block of coarse wood this way and that, running his long, slim fingers over the grain and allowing the light to play on the texture and color.

"Do you always find the duck?"

"Nope, sometimes it ain't in there. I'd think it was, but it wasn't. Mostly though, I find the duck. When I go looking for it, I usually find it."

I asked him to tell me more about the process he used.

"It's hard to talk about," he said. "But you're welcome to watch."

He began with a saw, cutting out the rough shape of a duck; and then he worked with knives to whittle away at the block.

"How long does it take to carve a duck?" I asked after 15 minutes of watching.

The old carver looked up at me, a sly smile spread

across his wrinkled face. "Takes a lifetime to carve a duck," he said. "Takes a lifetime."

He went on to explain that everything that had happened to him over the years—his love for the outdoors, his upbringing near a wildlife marsh, his hunting trips with his father—all influenced how he carved a duck. "And of course, some years of practice with these," he said as he pointed to his knives.

"You know," he said, not looking up from the wooden block, "a computer can carve a duck—in not much time either. But they all look the same—they are the same—one duck just like every other duck. But the ducks I carve are unique to the block of wood that gives them birth. I take into account the wood grain, the knots, the changes in hardness and softness of the wood. I'm constantly adjusting, constantly trying something new."

I came back a week later, and he said, "Here it is. The duck was in the block of wood. It just took a little more time than usual to find it."

—Source Unknown

When you find yourselves flagging in your faith, go over that story again, item by item, that long litany of hostility [Jesus] plowed through. That will shoot adrenaline into your souls!

—Heb. 12:3

2
Authentic Faith for Life's Details

The Man Who Prayed His Way into Heaven

Paul Hardy, a retired preacher, moved to Portland, Oregon, with his wife, Louella. His reputation as one with a gift of prayer intercession preceded him. In fact, one of his former pastors assured Pastor Denny at Portland that though Hardy was a bit noisy and a tad radical, he was authentic and his praying really brought results.

The Portland pastor, therefore, was puzzled when Mr. Hardy was cool to an invitation to attend the Saturday morning men's prayer breakfast. When the pastor pressed the matter, Hardy explained, "I've been to those prayer breakfasts before where there is a lot more breakfast than prayer."

"Ours is different!" explained Pastor Denny. "We meet at the church first and spend an hour in prayer on our knees, then go to breakfast."

Paul Hardy was delighted to hear that news. "Well," he exclaimed, "in that case I'll be there."

And he was. But not many weeks went by before the prayer meeting turned into an incredibly unforgettable event. As was our custom, we prayed around the circle, ending with the pastor. Paul Hardy prayed just before Pastor Denny. And how he prayed! With voiced raised and head looking heavenward, he literally pulled on the throne for the burdens of his heart.

When Hardy said "Amen," the pastor began to pray. During the pastor's prayer, Mr. Hardy suddenly called out in a very loud voice, "Oh God! Oh God!"

In a few moments, the pastor finished prayer, and we arose from our knees, but Paul Hardy didn't move. I slipped over and touched him and then said to the men, "He's gone!" Paul Hardy had actually prayed himself into the eternal Presence.

Soon the place was swarming with medics and other emergency people. To a man, they were moved when they heard that we had been having a prayer meeting. One man said with tears in his eyes, "What a wonderful way to go!"

Indeed, what a wonderful way to go—to be able to pray oneself into the presence of God for eternity.

—Richard S. Taylor

What I Learned at Little League

I watched Tommy, a friend of my son, Blake, strike out for about the 50th time that year. He must have hit the strikeout threshold because he threw his bat in the dirt and went back to the bench, sobbing uncontrollably. Blake was the next batter. He struck out, too, ending the game. The team had lost, as it had every Little League game that year.

Blake was quiet as we drove home. "It's just a game," I offered.

"Dad, I can't hit the ball," Blake burst out. "Do you know Tommy and me are the only guys on the team without a hit all year? At school, the other kids call us 'the strikeout kings.'"

"Tell you what," I said. "This week, before your last game, we're going to practice one thing: how to hit the ball."

I taught him everything my father and coaches had taught me—have a nice level swing, watch the ball meet the bat, and don't try to kill it.

In the final game of the season, Tommy got up to bat and smacked a double on the first pitch. Tommy was on second base, a place he'd never been in his life, beaming from ear to ear. I looked over to remind

Blake about what we'd worked on, but he was already striding toward the batter's box.

He barely missed the first two pitches. "This is going to be awful," I thought. But on the next pitch, Blake stuck out his bat and hit a home run. A Little League home run, that is, with a throw here, a throw there, a throw everywhere—but a home run all the same. As the two boys headed for home plate, the entire team came flying off the bench. The team's confidence soared, and it went on to win for the first and only time that season.

Driving home I exclaimed, "I'm so proud of you! A home run on your first hit! It just goes to show the value of good coaching."

Blake looked at me like I was crazy. "Coaching had nothing to do with it, Dad. When I saw Tommy hit the ball, I said to myself, 'If Tommy can do it, so can I.' And I did."

That's what the healthy church does for its people too.

—Roger Dow and Susan Cook

Help me the slow of heart to move
By some clear, winning word of love.
Teach me the wayward feet to stay,
And guide them in the homeward way.

—Washington Gladden

Wherever—The Adventure of the Quest

I used to laugh with a friend of mine about what we were going to be when we grew up. It seemed like a funny thing to say in college, but it probably became less and less amusing as the years rolled by. My answer for a long time was that I wanted to decide by the time I was 50 years old and then I wanted to be it for five years and then promptly retire. It is becoming apparent to me that I really do not know what I am going to be when I grow up. I cannot tell you what all I believe He wants me to be or where I think He is going to lead me. I can only pray that I will have the faith and courage to say whatever, wherever.

I hope I will be like the middle-ager who hit a double while playing baseball with his kids. He was on second. His breath was on first. But his heart was roaring around third toward home.

I know "wherever" is a reckless word. There are no halfway houses on the road to wherever. I have to use it guardedly. Even now, I have not gone far enough for it to be a word that is truly mine. But I would like to learn to live and believe so that "wherever" will hold no fears for me.

For one reason or another, I am not always a follower. Sometimes I am afraid to go. Sometimes my life is so good that I do not want to leave where I am. But when I have gone and when I have allowed it to become my word, I want to say to you unreservedly, wherever is worth going.

At times I have remained behind only to find myself surrounded with nothing. But sometimes I have left all to go with Him and I have known His everything. And I am convinced that if I would always go, I would always be glad.

The quest—
Wherever it takes you— go;
Whichever the task—do it.
Wherever the burden—accept it;
Whenever it calls—answer it;
Whichever the lesson—learn it;
However dark the path—follow Him,
Because *wherever He takes you,*
It is worth the going.

—*Bob Benson*

Pursue a righteous life—a life of wonder, faith, love, steadiness, courtesy. Run hard and fast in the faith.

—*1 Tim. 6:11-12*

What My Crippled Little Theologian Taught Me

Over the past nine years, my son, Grayson, has taught me great truths about life, love, and the Lord. At three and one-half months, a critical surgery saved his life, leaving him with a slight case of cerebral palsy. As a result, his motor skills are less than ideal, but his mind is magnificently intriguing. Sometimes when it comes to biblical understanding, my little theologian offers inspirational interpretations.

While attending Bible college, I was struggling to define the Trinity for my theology class. One morning as I was driving Grayson to kindergarten, I said, "Explain God the Father, the Son, and the Holy Spirit to me, buddy." He thought a moment as we pulled to the intersection. Then with confidence he replied, "It's like the traffic light, Dad. Three colors, but one light." My professor liked my son's interpretation much better than anything I could offer.

Bible college days can be a test of faith, especially for second-career students like me who have to work, raise a family, and study simultaneously. The days and nights are just not long enough to get everything done. During one of those especially tough periods in our lives, I guess my son, who was six at the time, sensed my struggles. That night as he prayed his bedtime prayers, he said, "Dear Lord. Daddy, Mom, Sis, and me still love You even if the sun's gone away."

Another night at prayers, Grayson, age seven, spoke these striking words, "Thank You, Father, for sending Your only forgotten Son, to die on my cross."

One of my son's most precious expressions about faith has become his unique trademark. It all began when he was two years old. One day I asked him how much he loved his daddy. With his hands stretched like wings beside him, he strained and declared, "Too much! I love my daddy too much!" Though he is now nine, he still answers "too much" whenever I ask him how much he loves me.

During this year's Easter season, I was preaching and attempting to illustrate just how much Christ loves us. Toward the end of the sermon I asked, "How much does Jesus love us?" Before I realized what was happening, I had spontaneously stretched my arms out to my side like I was hanging on the Cross. I recalled the image of my two-year-old son when he first communicated to me that way that he loved me—"too much." I envisioned Christ on the Cross, with His arms stretched out too. As the Lord Christ strained for my salvation, He proved just how much He really loved me. Only two words even come close to defining the depth of His devotion: He loved me "too much!"

Some may label truths I've learned from my young

son under childlike mistakes or early childhood development. Still, I wouldn't want to trade the lessons for anything.

In this day of cynical sophistication, we must not get beyond the truth as found in Christ. The words of the "love you too much" Savior warn and warm us, "Assuredly, I say to you, whoever does not receive the kingdom of God as a little child will by no means enter it" (Mark 10:15, NKJV).

—Kerry W. Willis

We're squinting in a fog, peering through a mist. But it won't be long before the weather clears and the sun shines bright!

—1 Cor. 13:12

Ye fearful saints, fresh courage take.
The clouds ye so much dread
Are big with mercy, and shall break
In blessings on your head.

—William Cowper

God Shows Up in the Strangest Places

Just as at the center of a hurricane there is stillness and above the clouds a clear sky, so it is possible to make a little clearing in the jungle of our human will for a rendezvous with God. He will always turn up, though in what guise and in what circumstances cannot be foreseen—perhaps trailing clouds of glory, perhaps as a beggar; in the purity of the desert or in the squalor of London's Soho or New York's Times Square. Once, in Times Square, I was glancing disconsolately, but also avidly, at the rows and rows of paperbacks, each with a lewd or sadist picture for its cover, and noticed by some strange accident my book on Mother Teresa, *Something Beautiful for God,* had gotten onto these sad shelves. Wondering how it could have happened, Herbert's beautiful lines came into my mind:

And here in dust and dirt, O Here
The lilies of His love appear.

For every situation and eventuality there is a parable if you look carefully enough.

—*Malcolm Muggeridge*

On Saying Grace

Jim was a Salvation Army bandsman who had been taught that God was interested in everyone's smallest needs. Testing the teaching came one day when he found himself in a restaurant. Having finished his meal, he discovered he had no money in his pocket.

Embarrassed, he braced himself for an ordeal of explanation with the cashier, and nervously waited his turn at the cash desk.

Suddenly, a hand grasped his shoulder. Apprehensively, Jim turned and found himself face-to-face with a man who was obviously the manager. The young bandsman wondered how to begin.

But the manager smiled and looking at the check in Jim's hand said, "That's all right. Your meal is on the house."

Jim swallowed hard. There was a surprised expression in his eyes. Then the manager explained, "You see, I'm a Christian too. When I opened this restaurant two weeks ago, I made up my mind that I would take no money from the first person I saw bowing his head and saying his grace before eating. You are the first."

Saying grace expresses the gratitude of the one who prays, but it is often a silent witness to those who see us pray.

—William G. Harris

A Word of Grace from an Alzheimer's Victim

The church youth group had just sung their final concert after traveling for 10 days, and they were tired and happy. But the group called Solid Ground had one more promise to keep before they would be on their way home. Leaving the sanctuary of their home church, they moved quickly like a colony of ants down the street to a nearby nursing home. They wanted to sing a song or two for one of their church members who could no longer attend services.

The church member was veteran minister and writer and broadcaster Milo Arnold—one of God's quiet, good men who increase the influence of the kingdom of God in every generation. Those who knew Arnold in his prime thought of him as an ideal pastor. Now a sad shadow of the person he had been, he sat slumped in his chair looking years older than he was. No one knew for sure whether he could make the connection between the young people and the church he loved so much in his more clear-minded days.

Realizing Pastor Arnold might not know them, the youth leaders still thought it would be a good service experience for the teens. And the visit turned out to be a more blessed experience of faith and hope and trust than they could have ever imagined.

After the choir sang a song or two, Milo Arnold sat very quietly. Then in a flash of insight he asked, "Could you sing 'Blessed Assurance'?"

So the group sang, "Blessed assurance, Jesus is mine! / O what a foretaste of glory divine!"

Then he asked them to sing it again, and how they sang: "This is my story, this is my song, / Praising my Savior all the day long."

The veteran pastor then sat up a little straighter. To their surprise, he transformed his wheelchair into a pulpit for a few moments. Though surprised, the tired teen choir became his eager listeners. One could hear a pin drop as residents and staff and teens felt enveloped in a holy hush.

"Never be bitter, young people," said the man of God with clear eyes and a quiet conviction in his voice. "For bitterness spoils the fruit of your lives, and rotten fruit isn't good for anything." He spoke of hard trials and the goodness of God's grace. As a victim of one of life's most cruel diseases, now he didn't seem to be a victim at all. In that moment of ministry, he became a living example of Fanny Crosby's hymn, "Perfect submission, all is at rest. / I in my Savior am happy and blest— / Watching and waiting, looking above, / Filled with His goodness, lost in His love."

God has many magnificent surprises along the Christian way.

God Loves Eccentricity and Excitement

Concerning some of the Salvation Army's ways and means to contact the masses for Christ, General Bramwell Booth once announced,

> We in The Army have learned to thank God for eccentricity and extravagance and to consecrate them to His service. We have men in our ranks who can rollick for the Lord. Often they have blundered, and occasionally they landed us in awkward places. Some of them have been very rough and uncouth and all that, but . . .
>
> Thank God for the dare-devils! They led us on the forward march. Their freedom of attack has brought, and still brings, within our reach the very people we want most.
>
> They have helped to keep us free from the shackles of respectability. They keep us passionate. So often even such a writer as H. G. Wells, after saying that our "shouts, clangor, trumpeting, gesticulations, and rhythmic pacing stun and dismay my nerves," yet can add, "I see God indubitably present in their excitements."

—William G. Harris

3

Transforming Obstacles into Opportunities

A Bridge over Troubled Waters That Reached to Iran

It was a usual Sunday morning in our Pasadena parsonage on November 4, 1979. My husband had left early to prepare for the sacrament of Communion. I was alone in the house, sitting by the fire reviewing my Sunday School lesson when the phone rang. It was my minister husband.

He said, "I have bad news." My heart skipped a beat as I thought about my mother visiting a son on the East Coast.

"Is it about Mother?" I asked.

"No," he said, "the Embassy in Iran has been overrun by terrorists and all the personnel are taken hostage." I understood how bad the news was—our older son, Gary, was a State Department Administrative Officer there.

"All?" I stammered with a lurching heart. "That means Gary!"

"Yes, I'm afraid so. Do you want me to come home?"

"No," I answered, "I'll be all right. You serve Communion as you planned."

I walked back to the fireplace. With shaking fingers I picked up a small radio and heard a local broadcaster trying to contact Tehran, Iran. He asked to speak to one of the hostages so the United States could be assured they were alive. The request was denied.

I turned the radio off, and thus began 444 days of uncertainty, agony, and learning to live on two levels—deep concern for our hostage son as well as the everyday demands of a busy life of ministry.

Scriptures from the Bible brought comfort to my spirit. Later, a strange quietness gripped me as I prayed, "Lord, what do I do next?"

The Father seemed to whisper, "Just do the next thing." I couldn't believe I was listening correctly.

"You don't mean to go to church, take Communion, teach my class, and worship as usual?" I stammered.

"Yes, go," the Inner Voice urged. "All will be well."

Since I had obeyed the promptings my whole life, I dared not disobey now.

With trembling hands, I dressed and drove to the church. As I sat at the Communion table and held the sacramental bread and cup in my hand, my prayer went across the time zones, 12 hours ahead of us, to the night in Iran where my son, as well as many others, were held prisoners. I prayed God to loose the bands and set the prisoners free—I felt assured that God heard me. A miracle of nearby grace filled my heart.

Hope in God kept me "doing the next thing" for over a year. I also had opportunity to discover the truth of a Scottish proverb a Sunday School member shared with me: "You don't thatch your roof when it's raining." Thank God my place of prayer gave me an inner sustenance that had been my constant shelter from the storms of life for many years.

On January 20, 1981, soon after President Reagan was inaugurated, the hostages flew out of Iranian airspace toward freedom and home. Later in Washington, D.C., watching Gary and his family descend the steps from the first plane into Andrews Air Force Base from West Point, my heart overflowed with thanksgiving and relief. The bridge of faith over troubled waters held us strong. God saw us through!

—Hazel C. Lee

I ask him that . . . you'll be able to take in with all Christians the extravagant dimensions of Christ's love. Reach out and experience the breadth! Test its length! Plumb the depths! Rise to the heights! Live full lives, full in the fullness of God.

—Eph. 3:17-19

Bravo, Lord, Bravo

Darlene Bee loved her work as principal of the New Zealand Summer Institute of Linguistics. A Ph.D., she analyzed the grammatical structure of a difficult tone language in Papua New Guinea—the Usufura language. She once described the complexity of Usufura verbs by making a chart for the forms of one verb. After copying about 7,000 forms onto a six-foot scroll, she gave up, estimating that there were 5,000 more.

Learned, shy, loving, she gave 14 years of self-forgetful service to this primitive tribe, living in bamboo huts, sitting by a smoking fire, studying by lantern often well into the midnight hours. She was the rare blend of laborer and artist. The master of words and language, she had the soul of a poet—a dreamer. She loved people with a quality that charmed them, and she loved the Lord God supremely, so that when she spoke or wrote, she brought God and the human beings who experienced her ministry together.

And then on April 7, 1972, she and six others were killed in a plane crash among the green ridges near Lae, Papua New Guinea. But now, years later, her dynamic Christ-centered life lives on in lines she wrote such as these:

From the magnificence of creation
to my small needs this day,
your word deserves
our applause;
far exceeding
our wildest imagining,
our fondest expectations,
our deepest desires,
they are perfect;
every detail
complete,
lacking in nothing,
and yet you go on and on
doing more and more,
promising still further
perfection,
greater majesty,
nobler doings.
Bravo, Lord, Bravo!
Encore! Encore!
More! More!

—John E. Riley

All you need to remember is that God will never let you down; he'll never let you be pushed past your limit; he'll always be there to help you come through it.

—1 Cor. 10:13

Freedom for Abused People

Face It, Forgive It, and Forge Ahead

For some of us, in our past,
There's pain and much abuse.
The hurt is great and scars are deep,
And we wonder, "What's the use?"

As anger boils down deep inside
From suffering in our past,
Sometimes we react in harmful ways,
Needing victory that will last.

We read and pray and seek advice,
Trying hard to cope.
"How do we handle our abusive past?
Is there any hope?"

"Face it, forgive it, and forge ahead,"
His Spirit comes to say.
We can recover from old hurts
And enter a brand-new day!

To face the hurt and forgive the wrongs
Is not an easy task.
But only then can we forge ahead
To real victory that will last.

—Norman Moore

Not Coincidences but "God-incidences"

Faith often contains an element of risk. Planting a new congregation in Southern California gives us lots of opportunities to risk for God. In our young congregation, we are learning to call our victories "God-incidences" instead of coincidences.

In the spring of 1992, as we prepared for starting this new church, we hand addressed our first mailing of 20,000 letters. I remember coming to the realization I would need to get the stamps, but I became weak kneed when the order totaled $6,000! In checking our budget, it meant we couldn't order the upholstered chairs *and* do the mailing. So, the stamps were ordered on a Friday, to be picked up on Monday. I went to our worship service that Sunday with our core group of 40 worshipers but never mentioned placing the order for 20,000 first-class postage stamps.

Then the God-incident happened. In checking the offering that afternoon, we found a check for $6,100! I immediately called the young contributor to be sure he had not placed the decimal in the wrong place. And then he told me his story.

That week his company had gone public on the stock market, and he had cashed out his company stock to buy their first house. The $6,100 was tithe on his earnings. He and his wife had sat down at their kitchen table on Wednesday night and had prayer as they wrote out their check. His words were, "Pastor, we have never written out a tithe check for $6,100!"

I told him I had never seen one before! They put the check in their tithe envelope for Sunday morning. And they had no idea of the invoice on Monday for $6,000 for the order of stamps. I said to him, "I don't know how, but some way God is going to reward you for this faithful stewardship."

He smiled and said, "He already has!"

On Thursday morning when he went into the office, his boss called him to schedule another annual review. He said, "But I've already had my review and raise for the year."

His boss said, "I know, but you're doing such good work and the company is growing so well, we thought you deserved another raise."

He said as his eyes filled with tears, "Pastor, they gave me an additional $15,000 a year raise!" Not a bad turnaround for less than 24 hours—from $6,100 to $15,000.

Of course, God doesn't multiply every faith-filled expression in such a remarkable way. But occasionally we experience God-incidences that remind us who He is when we risk for building His kingdom. As we dare to go out on a limb and take the risk, He is trustworthy.

—Jim Dorsey

Let the Winds Blow

The wind is almost at gale stage this morning. The tiny maple tree outside my window, clothed in summer foliage, appeared alternately amused and frightened by the treatment it received from the wind. Sometimes the little tree bowed and straightened gracefully or twisted grudgingly and resumed its poise without a smile. Sometimes the gust was so sudden and so violent that the little tree bent sharply, sprang back like a drawn bow, and seemed to look at me appealingly as though trying to say, "That was a narrow escape."

The little maple tree speaks to me as a parable of the humor and seriousness of life. Perhaps in theory the tree would prefer the motionless evening or the quiet morning when there is no strain and no unusual risk. But I think the tree may be partial to the gale. I am sure it sometimes enjoys the wind's rough play, for by resisting the wind's attempts to move it from its moorings, the roots of the tree are enabled to push more deeply into the soil. And the wind contributes to the toughness of the tree's fiber.

Like the tree, we dream of ease and security and inactivity and rest. We often think we would like to be left alone by everything or anyone that causes strain and inconvenience. But that is just a theory. Like the little maple tree, we are all strengthened by the conflict, strain, activity, and the gale more than the calm. Maybe we do our best when we are having lots of fun fighting the devil. But whether we admit to enjoying the storms or not, it is the strong wind that builds our stability, our rugged dependability, and enlarges our soul.

We need not be concerned whether the wind will come. The winds will blow—you can be sure of it. We can count on the storms, but our issue is to make sure every gale makes us surer, stronger, more stable, and satisfied in the development of our Christian character. Phillips Brooks, the great Boston preacher, warned we should not pray for tasks equal to our strength, but strength equal to our tasks.

It is well to remember that God is the Ruler of our strength and the Overruler of our storms. If our loving Father permits the wind to blow hard, that is proof for us that He is ready with strength to enable us to survive and to become stronger through each storm.

Let the winds blow.

—J. B. Chapman

The Seeker Whistled His Way to God

No man was too vile, hopeless, or sinful to be beyond the caring compassion of John Lyons, Irish missionary pioneer in Ceylon and early day Salvation Army officer in England.

Lyon's meetings were frequently disturbed by a local drunk who, nevertheless, was always made to feel welcome at "the Army." The day came when he unsteadily made his way to Christ. Lyons knelt by his side, his arms thrown around the man's shoulders in an embrace that is given to a long-lost brother.

Lyons prayed with him. Then he suggested that the man pray for himself.

"I don't know how to pray," came the helpless admission, "but I can whistle a hymn or two."

So a penitent soul whistled his way to the heart of God. His unique prayer was unquestionably heard and answered. It was the night of radical conversion. He was marvelously transformed and became an enthusiastic Salvationist.

—William G. Harris

Letting God Run His World

Brother Herman seems like an old familiar friend.

Herman, an impatient monk, was often critical of the actions of fellow monks and the leaders of the monastery. Nothing seemed right to him. He was always thinking of ways to rearrange the rituals, ways to streamline the divine worship services, and ways to improve living conditions. He suggested changes to make the monastery more efficient so it could care for more monks.

For Herman, worship services were often too long or too short. The meals were too rich or too plain. The chapel was either too hot or too cold. The halls were either too noisy or too quiet. Newcomers were either too well educated or too ignorant. The facilities were too old or too new. In short, Herman was interested in a revolutionary overhaul of the whole system of monastic life.

He lived in frustration because nothing suited him, and his campaigning for some change never seemed to produce results.

Finally, the kindly old abbot in charge of the

monastery felt obligated to speak to Herman. He said, "Brother Herman, I'm afraid you have a frustrating problem. You won't let God be God, and it's causing you ulcers."

Many Brother Hermans live outside monasteries. One may walk in your shoes or live at your address. Why not let God be God?

—A Parable from a Monastery

If our love were but more simple,
We should take Him at His word;
And our lives would be illumined
By the presence of our Lord.

—Frederick W. Faber

May our dependably steady and warmly personal God develop maturity in you so that you get along with each other as well as Jesus gets along with us all.

—Rom. 15:5

Singing in the Storms

I heard the story on radio, perhaps from Paul Harvey, and then from my old friend H. B. London. It was later published in Lucado's splendid book *In the Eye of the Storm*.

Chirpy, either a canary or parakeet, didn't know what hit him. One minute he was peacefully sitting in his cage; the next minute he was in the middle of a bird tornado.

His difficulties commenced when his owner decided to clean his cage with a vacuum cleaner. At the exact moment she put the vacuum attachment into his cage, the phone rang. When she turned to answer it, Chirpy was a goner, sucked up by the vacuum cleaner.

Quickly excusing herself from the phone call, the bird owner turned off the cleaning machine. Chirpy was alive but dazed when she opened the dirt bag.

The woman's mind went on emergency alert. Since Chirpy was covered with dirt, something had to be done. So she raced to the bathroom where she put the bird under the cold-water faucet. Then realizing that Chirpy was shivering and nearly drowned, she grabbed her hair dryer to dry and warm the bird.

Poor Chirpy—his world was completely shaken.

Think of all he went through—vacuum cleaner, darkness, whirling dirt and deafening noise in the dust bag, an icy shower that nearly drowned him, and then a near hurricane gale of hot air.

A few days after this mistreatment, a newspaper reporter called to ask how Chirpy was doing. The bird's owner replied with dismay, "Chirpy isn't singing much anymore. He just sits and stares."

Max Lucado's closing line says it all: "It's hard not to see why. Sucked in, washed up, and blown over . . . that's enough to steal the song from the stoutest soul."

Reach Beyond Your Comfort Zone

Men grind and grind in the mill of a truism,
and nothing comes out but what is put in.
But the moment they desert the tradition for
a spontaneous thought,
then poetry, wit, hope, virtue, learning, anecdote,
all flock to their aid.

—Ralph Waldo Emerson

"We Ain't Mad at Nobody 'Cuz Our Dad Died"

It was a picture-book story of a young Christian family headed by a firefighter from Kissimmee, Florida, named Flint Miller. He moved his family of four children to Colorado Springs so he could attend Bible college to fulfill a God-given conviction that he should change from saving lives to saving souls. Long before the dream could be realized, Flint was diagnosed with leukemia and lost his fight for life just a few days after his 32nd birthday.

The family move to Colorado brought many new experiences.

One story illustrates the adjustments: Since Flint loved horses, he found employment at the Broadmoor Hotel stables where the family lived in a mobile home near one of the riding trails. In a Colorado twist to "Goldilocks and the Three Bears," the Miller family left groceries on the table of the mobile home while they went on an errand. When they returned, they discovered bears had ransacked the mobile home and eaten the groceries.

The stories of grace and Christian support are even more amazing. The family of God lived up to its name. At first, it was almost impossible for anyone to accept the shocking leukemia diagnosis because Flint was such a he-man. Regrettably, the diagnosis was accurate and the prognosis bleak. Friends from area churches, the children's school, Flint's work, and the Bible college reached out to help, especially in caring for the children so Tammy could be with Flint as much as possible. Students at the college took over Tammy's job as cleaning engineer at the administration building so the work would get done and she could still receive the pay. Meals were brought in. Groceries were donated. People gave money for rent. Prayers were prayed—oh, how people prayed in churches nearby and far away. Friends fasted meals and sent cards of encouragement.

Tammy and Flint anguished over what to tell the children, who were frightened and confused. As days and weeks passed and round after round of chemotherapy failed, they continued to tell the children two things—Daddy's very sick and we trust God to take care of Daddy and us. Though they could not spend much time with their dad in the hospital because of the danger of infections, the children were devoted to him and kept his hospital room decorated with homemade get-well cards, notes, and pictures.

It seemed the medical reports were almost always bad and the fight was being lost. Flint's leukemia progressed rapidly, ruling out the option of waiting to find a suitable bone marrow donor. Soon a decision was made to try the experimental umbilical cord blood transplant. That meant chemotherapy and radiation in such strong doses that it would literally destroy Flint's own bone marrow.

After school was out, the children went for the summer to their grandparents in Tennessee and Florida. In spite of grim realities, they prayed and hoped, as did other members of the extended biological family and the family of God. Finally the doctors suggested the children be brought back to Colorado because the fight would soon be over. Flint died.

After all those weeks of our futile vigil, I had the both wonderful and awful experience of being with Tammy and the children and adult members of the family as they packed Flint's belongings at the hospital in Denver. The adults were dazed, and the children were huddled together on a sofa trying to fill the silence with a TV movie they did not really see. Funeral arrangements had to be made. Though the long struggle was done, no one knew how to deal with the reality.

On the way back to Colorado Springs, we stopped at a restaurant to feed the children lunch. Conversation was difficult and the silence deafening. What does one say to four children who have just experienced their father's death? But the children had to at least try to eat.

So I found myself seated at a restaurant table with the children—Adisha, Ciara, Matthew, and J. C.—and Tammy's mother, Pauline. To our surprise, Ciara wanted to pray over lunch. We all held hands as she prayed, "Dear God, we ain't mad at nobody 'cuz our dad's dead. We know he is in heaven with You, and he ain't sick anymore. Thank You for the food. Amen."

Through my tears I saw the childlike faith that Jesus proclaimed lived out before me that day, and I never want to forget it. The songwriter was right, "When answers aren't enough, there is Jesus."

—*Cindy Slaymaker*

This is the only race worth running. I've run hard right to the finish, believed all the way. All that's left now is the shouting—God's applause!

—*2 Tim. 4:7-8*

Sweet is the promise "I will not forget thee,"
Nothing can molest or turn my soul away;
Even tho' the night be dark within the valley,
Just beyond is shining one eternal day.

—Charles H. Gabriel

Win/Win of the Christian Life

My father faced the most pressing physical crisis of his life, and he probably realized the difficulties more than his family knew. Since his surgery to repair an aneurysm was to be done before daylight, my brother had to take Dad to the hospital before 5:30 A.M.

On the 50-mile drive, they had time to talk. Trying to keep things on a light side, my brother asked, "Are you ready for this great adventure?"

My father protested that the word "adventure" didn't fit. But his reply was built on long years of personal faith: "The way I have it figured out, regardless of how the surgery goes, I am in a win/win situation. If the surgery is a success, a few more years will be added to my life; and if it fails, I go into the presence of my Lord. Either way I win."

Dad's view sounds a lot like the apostle Paul's, who wrote nearly two centuries ago, "For to me, to live is Christ and to die is gain" (Phil. 1:21, NIV). My father didn't live through the surgery, but he did win life eternal, which is what he always dreamed of receiving from the Master. John Wesley was right: "Our people die well."

4
Love Enables, Endures, and Excites

Harry Is So Different Now

My teacher John Killinger told me this story: I remember the first Down syndrome child I ever knew. He was a boy of 11 or 12 in a parish in New England. He lived with his grandparents because the parents had not wished to cope with a special child.

Harry, the grandfather, had been a tough, aggressive businessman, and in the course of his life had not been especially good at personal relationships. But the loving qualities of the boy had done something to his personality. He had mellowed and changed and became more loving.

One day I stood with the grandmother, watching the grandfather and boy coming up through the meadow from the barn. They were holding hands and seemed to be having a wonderful time enjoying each other's company.

With a wonderful expression of profound thankfulness on her face, the grandmother said, "A little angel has touched our lives, and it is wonderful. Harry is so different now."

Dress in the wardrobe God picked out for you: compassion, kindness, humility, quiet strength, discipline. . . . wear love. It's your basic, all-purpose garment.

—*Col. 3:12-14*

Lord, take my life and make it wholly Thine;
Fill my poor heart with Thy great love divine.
Take all my will, my passion, self, and pride.
I now surrender; Lord, in me abide.

—J. Edwin Orr

Costly Love During Civic Tension

Dr. E. V. Hill, beloved inner-city pastor from Los Angeles, tells a life experience that sounds like a contemporary example of the incarnation of our Lord.

During the burnings, lootings, and riots of the 1960s, Pastor Hill spoke out against the attacks on human life, the stealing from store owners, and the destruction of property. As he spoke for God as best he understood the message, he was sometimes despised by people on both sides of the problem. During the worst part of the rioting, this kind of preaching brought threats to him, his church, and his family. However, the worse the situation became, the more obligated he felt to condemn the riots and fire and bloodshed.

One night, his phone rang, and his wife noticed how serious he was after he hung up. She knew something was wrong and asked, "What was that about?"

Trying to keep calm and to minimize the disruptions the situation was causing in his world and in his own life, Dr. Hill replied, "Oh nothing. It's not important."

But his answer caused his wife to keep pressing

him until he admitted, "They have threatened to blow up our car with me in it."

Late into the night hours, the Hills discussed how impossible it was to protect their car from wire bombings 24 hours a day. Finally they called it a day and turned in for the night—to sleep rather fitfully until morning.

Next morning, when Dr. Hill went into the kitchen, he noted his wife was not in the house. And he noticed the car was not in the carport when he looked outside. He became alarmed, but before he could decide what to do, his car rolled into the driveway with his wife at the wheel. Following their discussion the night before, she had decided to test-drive the car around the block to make sure it was safe for her husband to use later that morning.

"From that day," observed Hill, "I never asked my wife if she loved me." Her intensive love showed in her actions. That's the indelible pattern of the love of God in Christ—our Lord keeps showing us in such incredibly impressive ways how much He loves us. He demonstrates and inspires us to live love in action.

I'm so glad I learned to trust Thee,
Precious Jesus, Savior, Friend;
And I know that Thou art with me,
Wilt be with me to the end.

—Louisa M. R. Stead

You Become Real When a Child Loves You

They were in bed—again—after story time, bathroom, and prayers finally ended in fetching their favorite stuffed animals.

Chase went to bed feeling a little sick. No wonder. We found the half-empty tube of soothing citrus Blistik with teeth marks all over it under his bed. Earlier that day Tori had discovered that charcoal briquettes were edible. Imagine that—a new food group. Well, for the moment the house was quiet while Mommy graded a few papers. Daddy wandered listlessly around the house stepping on marbles and picking up stray Duplos. About the time we crawled under the covers, it began.

Chase heaved his supper all over his bed. About the time we got him cleaned up and calmed down, Tori decided it was her turn. This went on back and forth all night, but the worse of it was that by morning we were all sick.

So at 8:30 A.M., all four of us trudged into the doctor's office with varying degrees of fevers, sore throats, and runny noses. The doctor just smiled at us while envisioning the weekend in Bermuda he could now afford. We knew things were bad when

Chase started reminding us that it was "time for medicine."

Needless to say, the house was neglected for the time being. Tori no longer colored in her book but discovered instead how to make designs in the dust on the coffee table. We started thanking God for the VCR because it brought us 30 minutes of uninterrupted rest. But toward the end of the week, we flopped down on the couch beside Chase and Tori to watch *The Velveteen Rabbit*. Have you ever paid attention to the story about the velveteen rabbit when the skin horse explains what it means to be real:

> "Real isn't how you are made," said the Skin Horse. "It's a thing that happens to you. When a child loves you for a long, long time, not just to play with, but really loves you, then you become real."
>
> "Does it hurt?" asked the rabbit.
>
> "Sometimes," replied the Skin Horse. . . . "It doesn't happen all at once. You become. It takes a long time. That's why it doesn't often happen to people who break easily, or have sharp edges, or who have to be carefully kept. Generally, by the time you are Real, most of your hair has been loved off, and your eyes drop out, and you get loose in the joints and very shabby. But these things don't matter at all, because once you are Real you can't be ugly, except to people who don't understand."

There it is again: another reminder that even when

we wonder why Chase can sing the "obey song" but can't seem to do it, or when we think we'll scream if we have to wipe one more nose, those are the moments when Mommy and Daddy are most real.

On some days it's obvious that we are quite a bit shabbier than we used to be before the kids. A lot of Jerry's hair has been loved off, and Linda can find graham cracker slobber on almost every Sunday dress she owns. But we are more alive, more real than we used to be too.

And yes, those runny-nosed mess-makers are a life-affirming presence in our home. But they are echoes of the love that gives us life, for "God is love. Whoever lives in love lives in God, and God in him" (1 John 4:16, NIV). Now that's real. Try reading *The Velveteen Rabbit,* try applying the Bible to living and rejoicing in how your children make you real. Remember the part about hair and eyes and joints that the skin horse told the rabbit.

—Jerry and Lynda Cohagan

Throw yourselves into the work of the Master, confident that nothing you do for him is a waste of time or effort.

—1 Cor. 15:58

Has Anyone Told You You're Beautiful?

Father Jim was in charge of an orphanage and was an extraordinarily loving and caring man. All the children in the orphanage loved him dearly. Even after they grew up and established their own homes, the grown children came back to visit Father Jim. He was a magnet of love.

Jim was especially loved because he had a facility for accepting and cherishing in each child the very thing that boy or girl hated or most wished could be different. If a boy had unruly hair, Father Jim made it seem the most beautiful hair of all. For the boy with big feet that other children teased about when he tried to run, Father Jim praised until the strange feet became objects of pride and the other children wanted feet like that.

One day while Father Jim was in town buying supplies, a social worker brought a new child to the orphanage. The boy had a terrible birthmark covering half his face, and the boy had developed a disposition to go with the mark, for he was clearly unmanageable. He screamed and cursed at the social worker and at the other children.

Everyone wondered how Father Jim would respond to the new boy. Surely he could not find anything to extol. When Father Jim showed up in his battered old station wagon, everyone watched to see his reaction. The new child stood off by himself, defiant of everyone. Father Jim got out of his car with his usual joviality, and there were shouting and hugging as he greeted the children. Then they all grew silent and stood aside as he noticed the new boy.

"Hi," said Father Jim, "and who is this?"

"It's the new boy," the children shouted. Then the group fell silent, waiting to see what Jim would do. They would never forget what they saw.

Father Jim scooped the new boy into his arms and immediately planted a kiss right in the middle of the birthmark. Then he hugged the boy with all his might and said, "Welcome. You'll like it here."

Needless to say, the boy soon became a model child, and the other children accepted his birthmark as if it were something special, given by God. After all, Father Jim had kissed it, and that made it beautiful.

Think of yourself that way. God has kissed the part of you that you always despised. So it is with any human being that God has made when we see them with the eyes of God. We don't have to be attractive by Hollywood standards in order to be beautiful in the sight of God. We only have to be channels of His love in the world.

A Little Hope Goes a Long Way

I was taking a turn at counseling at the Sharing Place, a mission ministry for migrants in Toronto. The man who approached the table was perhaps the most hopeless looking man I had ever seen. He walked with a cane and looked very sick. He was perhaps in his 40s but seemed much older. His eyes reflected only despair.

I went through the usual questions with Jim. No, he didn't have any food. Yes, he needed a blanket. No, he didn't have a pillow. It was late October, and he didn't have a winter coat. We could help with those things, and we would.

The dialogue continued. "Jim, have you ever had anything to do with Sunday School or a church in your life?"

"Strange that you should ask that."

It wasn't strange to me. It was on our intake sheet, but since he thought it was strange, I asked him why.

"Because I'm an Anglican clergyman, but don't ask me where God is because I haven't the faintest idea."

"Would you like to tell me what happened?"

A shrug and then, "Both my kids died with cancer before the age of two. My wife said she couldn't serve a

God who would let that happen, and she left me. I started drinking. I was no good to my church. I left and got a job driving a cab. I kept on drinking, and I lost my health and my job, and that's what happened."

I do not have wisdom for these kinds of encounters with needy people, but God seemed to nudge me to pray. So I asked, "Jim, would it be all right if I prayed with you?"

Another shrug. "I don't care if you do or don't."

That wasn't no, but what should I pray about; I was impressed as if God was speaking, "Pray for hope. Jim needs a little hope."

I prayed simply that Jim would have a little hope stir in his inner life. Then I loaned him my reading glasses so he could see to use the point system we use for clothing choices at the Sharing Place and went on to counsel the next couple.

Sometime later, Jim returned the glasses. He had food, clothing, quilt, pillow, and the cane.

Then I said, "I'm almost finished here, Jim. If you wait a minute, I'll give you a drive home."

I helped him to the door of his very humble home and said good-bye. That night I asked my family to pray for Jim. I told them, "He's the most hopeless man I've ever met."

A week later, I received a call from another counselor at the Sharing Place. They asked, "Do you remember a man named Jim. He was in a week ago. He came back today and said the strangest thing. He said he didn't need food or clothing, but he wanted a little more hope. So I prayed he would have more hope."

Two months went by, and my husband and I were taking a man named Raj to the Sharing Place. He had escaped from certain death in Mozambique with just the clothes on his back. He needed winter clothes.

As we entered the Sharing Place, I saw a sharp-looking guy working with the coffee machine. Then I noticed him instructing some new volunteers, then working the files. I supposed he was some new volunteer I had never met until he turned around. It was Jim—a brand-new Jim. I decided not to remind him of the day we met, but a little later he stood beside me and quietly asked, "Do you remember me?"

"Yes, I remember you well."

"Do you remember I told you I didn't know where God was?"

"Yes."

"Would you believe God answered seven prayers of mine this week?"

He shared the answers to prayer and then said, "Do you know what made all the difference? You loaned me your glasses, and you gave me a drive home."

I felt humbled. These were such small acts of compassion, but they convinced a man someone cared. Someone prayed for hope. That made all the difference.

The story continues. Jim put in 12-hour days at the Sharing Place for eight more months, always giving his best, and his best was very good. He then felt he needed to return to his own family of churches. He did return and found a place of significant ministry there. And Jim often prays for others, "Lord, give us a little bit of hope."

—Marjorie Osborne

Getting Ready to Live

First I was dying to finish high school and start college.
And then I was dying to finish college and start working.
And then I was dying to marry and have children.
And then I was dying for my children to grow old
enough for school so I could return to work.
And then I was dying to retire.
And now, I am dying . . . and suddenly
I realize I forgot to live.

—Anonymous

Answers to Life's Riddles

We hear answers to life's problems and life's questions in the echoing, blessing, pulsating rhythm of Paul's declaration: "Now abideth faith, hope, charity, these three" (1 Cor. 13:13, KJV). There you have the answers to life's tests. Those answers abide.

"Now abideth faith" in Christ. We want to depend on people and on familiar situations. But life knocks the props from under every one of us; that is part of growing up physically and spiritually. The teaching process for this lesson is usually more or less gradual, but in some devastating experience life is torn up by the roots or goes to pieces under us. Then we can sing, "When all around my soul gives way, / He then is all my Hope and Stay." That's a dependable answer. Faith abides and is proved by obedience through the fog and darkness.

"Now abideth . . . hope" in Christ. We want to see what is ahead, but life is full of confusing blind alleys. Sooner or later we shall run into a situation that is impossible, a tangle that seems insoluble, a mess that we have caused, or a failure that is almost unforgivable.

What then? Discouragement? Fear? Despair? Turn fatalist or cynic? No, there is hope in what appears hopeless. The God of hope is named Providence. God is for you. Let Him show you the way out. Let Him shape your plans. No situation is hopeless, because Christ has died and risen and gone to heaven, interceding for us. There is no dead end for the one who holds on to Christ through thick and thin, through victory and victimizing. We have hope in Christ.

"Now abideth . . . love" in Christ. The greatest of these three is love. Love is positive, not negative. It is dynamic, a driving urge. It gives you more than the stoic's "grin and bear it" to meet life. It gives you the Kingdom to put first and a world of people to bless with Christ's Golden Rule. Love is omnipotent. In saving and blessing others, you save and bless yourself. Try loving your enemy and pushing your rival's interest.

Some say the world is going to pieces around us. It surely looks that way. But in the stirring shipwreck story of the Book of Acts, Paul proved what abides. He held to faith and hope and love. He said, "I believe in God"; "Be of good cheer"; "There shall be no loss of anyone's life"; "They escaped all safe to land."

The answer for all life's knowns and unknowns, for all life's uncertainties and certainties, too, is found in the big three—"abideth faith, hope, and love."

—*Bertha Munro*

Strange Helper for Math Lessons

Somewhere I heard the story about a fourth grade or fifth grade boy who was having trouble understanding his math lessons in school. The teacher nearly despaired and wondered what the next step in her instruction could possibly be.

Then one day the boy came to class with every answer right on his math lesson. The teacher knew that his parents were not capable of helping him very much, so she was very curious about how he was able to get all the right answers. She was amazed at his improved understanding.

She asked the boy about the change. To her amazement, the boy thought it was no big deal that he was finally understanding his math. He simply said, "My neighbor has been helping me." That sounded plausible, but then he thought to give his neighbor's name: "Mr. Einstein."

The shocked teacher didn't know how to reply, but we have one that is greater than Einstein to help us with life.

Having nothing, [yet] having it all. —*2 Cor. 6:10*

In Giving We Receive

A statue of Francis of Assisi stands in San Francisco, the city by the bay bearing his name. It is cast out of melted-down handguns. How amazing that Francis's influence continues after 800 years.

Giovanni Francesco Bernardone was born in 1182 into the home of a wealthy textile merchant in Assisi, Italy. As a young man, he spent a year as a prisoner of war and later experienced a lengthy illness. These two difficult periods apparently helped him establish a new relationship with God and with nature.

One writer said of him, "As a young man, Francis had a particular distaste for lepers. While riding horseback one day, he encountered a leper standing beside the road. Initially repulsed, then feeling a strange surge of compassion, Francis dismounted and put money into the man's hands. 'More is required of you,' said a small voice in Francis' heart. In a dramatic gesture he would later regard as a turning point in his life, Francis kissed the leper." From that time on he saw himself as having a special bond with the poor, hurting, and disadvantaged.

To this day, believers of nearly every doctrinal persuasion sing Francis's prayer:

Lord, make me an instrument of Thy peace. . . .
Where there is hatred, let me sow love. . . .
For it is in giving that we receive; . . .
It is in dying that we are born to eternal life.

Francis teaches so well that in serving others we receive more than we give. Love means getting close to human need—getting dirty and hurting and sometimes suffering with those who suffer. Theologians call it incarnation. Jesus and Francis call it love. Everyone can enrich the personal journey by giving and receiving Christ's kind of love.

In heav'nly love abiding,
No change my heart shall fear;
And safe is such confiding,
For nothing changes here.
—Anna L. Waring

Now do what you've been taught. School's out; quit studying the subject and start living it!

—*Col. 2:7*

5 Serving Creates Its Own Satisfactions

Be Used by a Great Purpose

This is the true joy in life, being used for a purpose recognized by yourself as a mighty one.

. . . being a force of nature instead of a feverish, selfish little clod of ailments and grievances complaining that the world will not devote itself to make you happy.

I am of the opinion that my life belongs to the whole community and as I live it, it is my privilege to do for it whatever I can.

I want to be thoroughly used up when I die, for the harder I work the more I love. I rejoice in life for its own sake.

Life is no brief candle to me; it is a sort of splendid torch which I've got a hold of for the moment, and I want to make it burn as brightly as possible before handing it on to future generations.

—*George Bernard Shaw*

O the pure delight of a single hour
That before Thy throne I spend,
When I kneel in prayer and with Thee, my God,
I commune as friend with friend!

—Fanny J. Crosby

Each person is given something to do that shows who God is: Everyone gets in on it, everyone benefits. All kinds of things are handed out by the Spirit, and to all kinds of people!

—*1 Cor. 12:7*

Serving Always Connects Us to Jesus

Mother Teresa and her sisters of the Missionaries of Charity have proven that the stubborn and tireless energy of a dedicated few can redefine the meaning of service for an entire generation. Contrasting the way he responded to the poorest of the poor in India to the way Mother Teresa responds, journalist Malcolm Muggeridge observed:

> I ran away and stayed away. Mother Teresa moved in and stayed. She, a nun, rather slightly built, with a few rupees in her pocket; not particularly clever, or particularly gifted in the art of persuasion. Just with this Christian love shining about her; in her heart and on her lips. Just prepared to follow her Lord, and in accord with His instructions to regard every derelict left to die in the streets as Him; to hear in the cry of every abandoned child, even in the tiny squeak of a discarded fetus, the cry of the Bethlehem child; to recognize in every leper's stumps the hands that once touched sightless eyes and made them see, rested on distracted heads and made them calm, brought back health to sick flesh and twisted limbs.

She is aware that these dying and derelict men

and women, these lepers with stumps instead of hands, these unwanted children, were not pitiable, repulsive or forlorn, but rather dear and delightful; as it might be, friends of long standing, brothers and sisters. How is it to be explained—the very heart and mystery of the Christian faith? To sooth those battered old heads, to grasp those poor stumps, to take in one's arms those children consigned to dustbins, because it is His head, as they are His stumps and His children, of Whom it was said that whosoever received one child in His name received Him.

—Malcolm Muggeridge

We have plenty of hard times that come from following the Messiah, but no more so than the good times of his healing comfort—we get a full measure of that, too,

—2 Cor. 1:5

Like the sunshine after rain,
Like a rest that follows pain,
Like a hope returned again,
*Is the peace that Jesus gives.**

—Haldor Lillenas

When a Prayer Turned into Evangelism

A duty-free shop in the Aerolineas Argentinas terminal in Buenos Aires' Ezeiza Airport was where it began.

I was tired. Nine days at an international prayer and evangelism institute had inspired and exhausted me. But here came Raul.

"Excuse me, señor, but este mate mug is overpriced much."

I smiled politely. "Oh, which one should I buy, then?"

And that's how we met. Raul was on his way to Los Angeles as well—on my flight. We struck up a conversation. Middle-aged, athletically built, this soft-spoken Argentine offered his story to me in broken English. A wife recovering from major surgery, three children, parents to look after, no good work for him as an electrical technician. So, back to San Jose, California—Raul's third trip in four years—to earn money, retain his work visa, sell a car.

I listened with a bit more than half an ear. Inside I prayed, "OK, God. I'm trying a little experiment. Let's see if what I learned this week actually works . . ."

". . . and I pray to God she will be OK while I'm gone—probably six months," Raul offered.

Raul had my full attention again. He described his Catholic roots, and I sensed God urging me to say the words that were hard for me to say to a stranger, "Can I pray for you, Raul?"

He said yes, and I did. Something happened: he shed a tear. He didn't speak, but I looked into his eyes; they communicated fear, pain—internationally spoken languages. It was a simple prayer, but God was to use it like a can opener.

Time to board. We found our seats, and I settled in for the long flight to Mexico City where we were to lay over. As we crossed the Andes, swinging north out over the Chilean coast, I wrote in my journal, "Lord, prove to me that prayer is evangelism."

Soon after, Raul made his way down the aisle, settling into the seat next to me. We talked for several hours, off and on. God's Spirit gave me words like easy gifts. I handed them to Raul—little snippets of Scripture, my own simple story—and he received them.

Somewhere over Baja Del Sur, Raul received the Grand Prize—personal faith in Christ. I said, "Would you like to pray with me to begin a new life in Christ?"

He said, "Yes—but in Spanish." So I prayed in English, and Raul repeated in Spanish. I left the translation in God's hands.

Raul returned to his seat, and I opened my little green journal. I read my last entry, ready to begin writing where I had left off.

"Lord, prove to me that prayer is evangelism."

He had.

Something caught in my throat. After a minute or two, I discreetly brushed my eyes and, staring out at the starry night, realized that I would never be able to pick up where I had left off.

—*Kyle Duncan*

He giveth more grace when the burdens grow greater;
He sendeth more strength when the labors increase.
To added affliction He addeth His mercy;
To multiplied trials, His multiplied peace.

His love has no limit;
His grace has no measure.
His power has no boundary known unto men.
For out of His infinite riches in Jesus,
*He giveth, and giveth, and giveth again!**

—Annie Johnson Flint

Love Colors Service Beautiful

It was almost time for the service. If only I could make real to that crowd God's love through Christ. As I hurried up the front steps into the church, a little girl stepped in front of me. I spoke to her and started to go on, but she pressed against my hand.

"I brought you something," she said rather haltingly. Now I saw the crude bouquet of flowers. Some of them looked more like weeds. They were tied with a stringy ribbon in a little girl's bow. "I picked them just for you." Her eyes were dancing.

"Oh, thank you, honey." And I took them—still trying to push my way into the church. Then I caught the look in her eyes. The light was turning to tears as she added, "I made the corsage for you to wear. Aren't you going to put it on?" For one fleeting moment I saw myself wearing the weedlike, homemade bouquet. What would people think? Then I looked into her eyes again—even into her heart—and saw the love that prompted the action.

"Yes, honey, I'm putting it on right now. It is beautiful!"

As I pinned that little girl's corsage on my shoulder, I thought of the times God had taken my crude attempts to serve Him. In the service, I shared with the congregation something about the flowers I was wearing. And without spelling it out, the lesson came shining through.

—Mary E. Latham

Cleaning Up My 20-Foot Swath

I was frustrated about the litter left about our campus but did almost nothing about it. Finally, instead of choosing seething anger, hot letter writing, or demonstrations, I chose a 20-foot swath. I decided to take ownership. I would be the solution. I did not tell anyone about this; it was probably against some rule anyway.

I decided that I would be responsible for the environmental quality of this 20-foot swath—a stretch of lawn between the tennis courts and the soccer field where I walked each day. I couldn't care for the whole campus. That is someone else's problem. But each day, going from and to my car, I picked up litter.

At first, it was as much as I could conveniently carry. Then I made a game of it, limited my picking to 10 items each way. It was an exciting day when I realized I was picking up faster than "they" were littering. Finally, the great day arrived when I looked back on my 20-foot swath of lawn and it looked perfectly clean.

I have done this for several years now. Has general campus appearance changed? Not much! Have litterbugs stopped littering? No!

Then why bother if nothing has changed? That's

my secret. My 20-foot swath has changed, and I have changed! That five-minute walk is a high point of my day. Instead of fussing and stewing and storing up negative thoughts, I begin and end my workday in a positive mood. My perspective is brighter. I can enjoy my immediate surroundings—and myself—as I pass through a special time and space.

I now practice a discipline of leaving each time-space capsule of my life a little better than I find it. Each personal contact, each event, each room I enter becomes a small challenge. I want to leave it improved, but more important, I improve in the process. And thereby, maybe my having been there will make life better for someone else even as I make life better for me.

—Author Unknown

Consecrate me now to Thy service, Lord,
By the pow'r of grace divine.
Let my soul look up with a steadfast hope,
And my will be lost in Thine.

There are depths of love that I cannot know
Till I cross the narrow sea;
There are heights of joy that I may not reach
Till I rest in peace with Thee.

—Fanny J. Crosby

Weary from Fruit Bearing

An old saint once told me about a small peach tree in her yard. It seemed the tree was pruned and watered and fed by the owner. Annually the little tree gave every ounce of energy to bear peaches. During fruit-bearing season, the branches had to be propped up to keep the fruit from breaking them.

After the peaches were harvested, the tree seemed to go into a period of exhaustive rest until fall, and then it appeared dead all winter. The tree was weary from fruit bearing—it had given itself to its main reason for being. Healthy growth and strong branches and new leaves were all produced for the main reason of bearing fruit.

Could it be some Christians are periodically weary from fruit bearing? Maybe what looks like apathy and disinterest and laziness is really weariness that calls for a rest before more fruit can be grown.

No matter what I say, what I believe, and what I do, I'm bankrupt without love.

—1 Cor. 13:3

6
Allowing Faith to Crowd Secular Values

"Aren't They All Our Children?"

Senator Sam Nunn told a story that happened in Bosnia. A little girl was hit by a sniper in the tragic conflict in the middle of Sarajevo. At the moment of the shocking pain, a reporter dropped his pencil and pad and "rushed to the man who was holding the child and helped them both into his car.

"As the reporter stepped on the accelerator, racing to the hospital, the man holding the bleeding child said, 'Hurry, my friend, my child is still alive.' A moment or two later, 'Hurry, my friend, my child is still breathing.' A moment later, 'Hurry, my friend, my child is still warm.' Finally, 'Hurry. Oh my God, my child is getting cold.'

"When they got to the hospital, the little girl had died. As the two men were washing the blood off their hands and clothes, the man turned to the reporter and said, 'This is a terrible task for me. I must go tell her father that his child is dead. He will be heartbroken.' The reporter was amazed. He looked at the grieving man and said, 'I thought she was your child.'

"The man looked back and said, 'No, but aren't they all our children?'"

Then Senator Nunn reminded his hearers, "Yes, they are all our children. They are also God's children as well, and He has entrusted us with their care in Sarajevo, in Somalia, in New York City, in Los Angeles, in my hometown of Perry, Georgia, and here in Washington, D.C."

Your town must be added to the list. And your church belongs on the list too.

—From *It Takes a Church Within a Village*

Jesus loves me! this I know,
For the Bible tells me so.
Little ones to Him belong;
They are weak, but He is strong.

Jesus loves me! this I know,
As He loved so long ago,
Taking children on His knee,
Saying, "Let them come to Me."

—Anna B. Warner and David R. McGuire

The Power of Little People

Years ago when Andrew Young was U.S. Ambassador to the United Nations, he was walking down a hall in that mammoth building on his way to a press conference. Reporters and photographers dogged his steps, shouting questions and comments at his back. But Young kept walking.

As he moved down the hall, he spotted an old man carrying two brooms near the elevators. The ambassador stopped to shake the janitor's hand. With a look of pride, the old man advised Young, "You go get them, boy. Do us proud."

At that moment, Young smiled and said to an aide, "It's people like him that make me able to put up with this foolishness."

Every Christian leader, whether in a secular or religious assignment, knows the power of common people to inspire, to intercede, and to energize their achievement. The authentic leader can't get along very long without the strength of ordinary people to vitalize the cause they represent. And who would want to try—the confidence of our elders energizes our efforts.

—Robert Fleming

The Problems Vital Religion Produces

John Wesley, founder of Methodism and grandfather and great-grandfather of many more recent religious movements, wrote about the problems authentic personal faith sometimes produces:

> Wherever riches have increased, the essence of religion has decreased in the same proportion. Therefore, I do not see how it is possible in the nature of things for any revival of religion to continue for long. For religion must necessarily produce both industry and frugality, and these cannot but produce riches. But as riches increase, so will pride, anger, and love of the world in all its branches. How then is it possible that Methodism, that is a religion of the heart, though it flourishes now as the green bay tree, should continue in this state?
>
> For the Methodists in every place have grown diligent and frugal; consequently they increase in goods. Hence, they proportionately increase in pride, in anger, in the desire of the flesh, the desire of the eyes, and the pride of life. So, although the form of religion remains, the spirit is swiftly vanishing away. Is there no way to prevent this—this continual decay of pure religion?

And the question still needs to be answered.

Really Seeing Life

Helen Keller, the blind and deaf woman, was asked what she would choose if she could be given three days to see. She answered,

> On the first day I would want to see the people whose kindness and companionship have made my life worth living. I would call in my friends and look for a long time into their faces. I would also look into the face of a new baby. I would like to see the many books which have been read to me.
>
> The next day I would get up early to see the dawn. I would visit a museum to learn of man's upward progress in the making of things. I would go to an art museum to probe the human soul by studying paintings and sculptures.
>
> The third morning I would again greet the dawn, eager to discover new beauties in nature. I would spend this last day in the haunts of persons where they work. I would stand at a busy corner, trying hard to understand something of the daily lives of persons by looking into their faces and reading what is written there.
>
> On the last evening I would go to the theater and see a hilariously funny play so as to appreciate the overtones of humor in the human spirit. Yes, by God's light in Christ, seeing what matters and beholding the extraordinary in the commonplace.

The Power of One Act to Change History

On December 1, 1955, in Montgomery, Alabama, Rosa Parks, tired from a full day of work as a seamstress, violated a Jim Crow law by refusing to give up her seat on the bus to a white person. She was put in jail, and her imprisonment set off a 381-day bus boycott by her people. Many think her decision sparked the Civil Rights Movement in the United States. Her decision also pressured the court system to proclaim that segregation on public transportation is illegal.

Reflecting on those happenings nearly 40 years later, Rosa Parks said,

> I did not get on that bus to get arrested; I got on the bus to go home. Getting arrested was one of the worst days in my life. It was not a happy experience. Since I have always been a strong believer in God, I knew that He was with me and only He could get me through the next step.
>
> I had no idea that history was being made. I was just tired of giving in. Somehow, I felt that what I did was right by standing up to the bus driver. I did not think about the consequences. I knew that I could have been lynched, manhandled, or beaten. I chose not to move. When I made that decision, I

knew that I had the strength of my ancestors and God with me.

Thousands of simple acts done in the name of righteousness have changed history. Persistent personal righteousness might transform contemporary society.

Strange Judgment of Christians

After living in London's slums and offering sacrificial ministry for years to the needy people in every possible way, a mission worker was robbed late one night. The thief demanded money and the man's wallet but wanted still more.

During the encounter, the robber either fell or was pushed. He hissed with anger, "That wasn't a very Christian thing for you to do, was it?"

Too often, nonbelievers offer harsh, unreasonable judgments of Christians. What a silly process. But maybe it shows there is still some small awareness in the culture about what a Christian is supposed to do and be.

The Clash of Hopes

Kenny was one of the most affable men I ever knew. So imagine my surprise when he came to my study one day and announced he would shoot himself if I didn't give him the right answer.

"Is this a joke?" I asked him. He flew into a rage.

"Grace is pregnant. I want you, as her rabbi, to tell her that she is allowed to abort the child."

"Why would she want to do that?"

"Because I am forty-five years old. I have three grown children, and I am tired. All my life I've wanted time to travel, enjoy, not be tied down. Now this. No. I'm not going to wait another ten years. I have a right. I earned the right. You hear me, Rabbi?"

"Does Grace want the baby?"

"Yes, but she'll agree if you give her permission."

"I will not," I said. "Listen, Kenny. You have three gifted children, each of whom you love. Now your wife is willing to bear the pain of giving birth to another. She wants the child and she deserves it."

He glowered. Then he pulled a handgun out of his breast pocket. I was startled. He's gone berserk, I thought. He waved the gun at me, then at himself. What did he intend to do?

A moment later, he put the gun back into his pocket. "I'm serious about this," he said, "very serious. If you don't tell her to abort the baby, I will leave here, get on the Ventura Freeway, and blow my brains out."

I stared at him. A kaleidoscope of pictures was whirling through my head—of blood and death and crying children and funerals and guilt. Still, I felt that no one can hold a family or a religion hostage this way. I was not responsible for this man's irrational acts, and I doubted that he would take his life over the birth of a baby.

"Kenny, if that's the way you feel, you're going to have to kill yourself," I said.

He fled my home in eye-popping rage, slammed the front door, ran to his car, and drove away.

Seven months later, during services, a note was brought to my pulpit. It read, "Please announce the birth of a baby girl to Kenny and Grace." When the service was over, Kenny was waiting for me. "It was easier to wait than to die," he said. I thanked God. I thought to myself that philosopher Friedrich Nietzsche was right after all. He once said, "What doesn't kill you, makes you stronger." In a strange way I became stronger, too.

Kenny had a clash of hopes. Until Grace became pregnant this last time, his hopes for his family had been realized, and the grand hope lay ahead—to have it all and yet to be free. But some hopes must be put on hold. Kenny was right about a lot of things in life, "It was easier to wait than to die." And his life was enriched by the young child in ways beyond his wildest dream.

—Maurice Lamm

A Hush in the Rush

How to get the "hush" in the "rush," that is our problem! For by far the busiest Christmas bell is on the cash register or the computer. It tinkles away while people waddle from counter to counter like "animated Christmas trees," as Sangster once said. Indeed, more like forests of human Christmas trees. Nudging branches and heads reaching for air in the rare atmosphere of Dillards or Target or Wal-Mart. And all the while that bell keeps a-ringing! And from invisible overhead stereophonic archangels there throbs the false promise,

Silent night! holy night!
All is calm, . . .

So you go "round and round" like the beat music—and just as "beat"—hoping against hope that you'll come up with that something really original for her and him; such as

A partridge in a pear tree

. . . .

Two turtledoves

. . . .

Eight maids a-milking

So you wonder as you wander down the crowded aisles . . . dusting the remote corners of your mind for ideas and the not-so-remote corners of your wallet for something to use in place of money. And all the while hypnotic fingers lure you to this dinky like thingamajig eloquently described as "nice!" But hold your purse strings a bit; here's something better; at least its called "exquisite." And after all, it is exquisite, this neat, sweet, little, red leather coat with blue pussy willows! Or this "exquisite" evening gown with sequins—for your French poodle.

But now the stereophonic archangels have changed their tune; now it's

How silently, how silently
The wondrous Gift is giv'n!

How in the world did it come to this? For in all the world it has. The only Christmas "rush" is the real story that began and ended with the quickstep of the sandaled shepherds as they clattered down Bethlehem High Street—and no lights! And no holly boughs; and no flying cherubs with St. Tristan faces; and no Open until Midnight signs. For when God came, He tiptoed into history through the back door. He put His revolution into a cradle. True, it "rocked the world," but not that night. To split history, He used infant hands.

They all were looking for a King.
To slay their foes, and lift them high;
Thou cam'st a little baby thing
That made a woman cry.

The raucous noise from the saloon had nothing to

do with Jesus. "Mine Host," a good fellow and all that jazz, was up beyond his ears in the rush, but not the Christmas one.

Try finding your own hush in the rush.

—T. C. Mitchell

Rise up, O Church of God!
Have done with lesser things.
Give heart and mind and soul and strength
To serve the King of Kings.

—William P. Merrill

Keep a firm grasp on both your character and your teaching. Don't be diverted. Just keep at it.

—1 Tim. 4:16

MORE *Come to the Water Brook* BOOKS TO COME?

Stories, songs, and scriptures for this book come from wonderfully gifted storytellers who eagerly shared experiences from their lives. We labored hard and long over the decision as to what could be left out in order to meet publishing limitations. If this book is well accepted, author and publisher would like to consider doing one or more future volumes in a Come to the Water Brook Series.

If you think another volume would strengthen hope, encourage faith, and fuel devotion, let us hear from you.

Let us also hear about your favorite inspirational happenings from your life, your family, or your neighbors that we might include in future books.

Please enclose a copy of those stories with your letter, and mail to this address:

Neil B. Wiseman
Come to the Water Brook Series
Beacon Hill Press of Kansas City
P.O. Box 419527
Kansas City, MO 64141

Stories should be not more than 500 words, typed and clearly marked with the name, address, and phone and/or fax number of the sender. Stories cannot be returned, so storytellers should keep copies of matter they send.